BEN YARMOLINSKY

FOUR PIECES FOR PIANO

ED-3383
First Printing: November 1992

G. SCHIRMER, Inc.

Distributed by
 Hal Leonard Publishing Corporation
7777 West Bluemound Road P.O. Box 13819 Milwaukee, WI 53213

Dedicated to Markus Seibel

I. PASTORALE

Ben Yarmolinsky

II. NOCTURNE

Ben Yarmolinsky

III. DANCE

Ben Yarmolinsky

FINALE

Ben Yarmolinsky